EPILEPSY GUIDE BOOK

LIVING A NORMAL LIFE WITH EPILEPSY

By

Dr. James M. Thomas

CONTENTS

ILLUMINATING THE PATH TO UNDERSTANDING EPILEPSY

INTRODUCTION

A silent conflict is taking place in the shadowy recesses of the night. Fighting an undetectable enemy is difficult because the condition strains both the body and the psyche. Nobody is immune to the unpredictable spells cast by epilepsy, a complex neurological illness, which affects many lives. But fear not, for within these pages shines a beacon of hope and understanding, revealing a road to triumph over adversity.

Welcome to a fascinating voyage through the complex world of epilepsy. This journey will dispel myths, expose new information, and empower both patients and the people who care for them. More than just a book "epilepsy guide book, living a normal life with Epilepsy " serves as a companion, a roadmap, and a source of motivation. With each, we encourage you to explore the depths of understanding, sympathy, and resiliency in every chapter.

You will come across remarkable bravery stories, investigate ground-breaking scientific discoveries, and learn the keys to taking charge in these pages. We'll travel through the illustrious past of epilepsy, into the mysterious depths of the brain, and beyond, where cutting-edge treatments and scientific advancements shine as glimmering beacons of hope.

This book will arm you with knowledge, allay worries, and fuel a flame of determining whether you are a warrior waging your battle with epilepsy, a caregiver offering unflinching support, or a curious soul seeking insight. Let's work together to solve riddles, dispel myths, and change the way the world views epilepsy. So, dear reader, let's begin this life-changing journey together because you will learn from these pages that epilepsy is not who we are; rather, it is only one chapter in our remarkable tale of resiliency, bravery, and unwavering spirit. By illuminating the way to triumph as a team, we will each individually liberate our power.

CHAPTER 1

A HISTORICAL OVERVIEW OF EPILEPSY

Epilepsy has a lengthy and interesting history that goes back thousands of years. Recurrent seizures, which are a hallmark of epilepsy, are brought on by aberrant electrical activity in the brain. Epilepsy has been misunderstood, stigmatized, and the subject of several interpretations and therapies throughout history. Let's examine the significant turning points in epilepsy history:

historic civilizations

In ancient civilizations including Mesopotamia, Egypt, and Greece, epilepsy was first mentioned. In ancient societies, epilepsy was frequently linked to supernatural or divine causes, and those who had it were thought to be under the influence of demons or gods.

Hippocrates and the Humoral Theory:

Hippocrates, a Greek physician, advocated a more scientific approach to treating epilepsy in the fifth century BCE, rejecting the notion that it was a spiritual illness. According to him, epilepsy is a brain condition that results from an imbalance of the four body humor (blood, phlegm, black bile, and yellow bile).

Roman times: Greek theories had a significant impact on Roman knowledge of epilepsy. Galen, a Roman physician, elaborated on Hippocrates' theories and suggested that epilepsy was brought on by too much phlegm in the brain.

The Middle Ages: Epilepsy remained connected to paranormal ideas during this era. Epileptics were frequently thought to be under the control of demons, which contributed to societal shame and discrimination.

Exorcisms and other religious rites were used in some therapies.
The Age of Enlightenment and the Modern Era: In the 18th century, epilepsy was better understood from a scientific and medical standpoint. The concept of focal seizures and their relationship to certain regions of the brain were introduced by doctor John Hughlings Jackson, who made substantial advancements to our understanding of epilepsy.

The early 20th century saw the invention of electroencephalography (EEG), which completely changed how epilepsy was diagnosed and researched. Hans Berger, a German psychiatrist, recorded the first human EEG in 1924, allowing for the detection of abnormal brain wave patterns associated with epilepsy.

Epilepsy treatment alternatives became available once antiepileptic medicines (AEDs) were discovered in the middle of the 20th century. The first contemporary AED was phenytoin (Dilantin), which was introduced in 1938. Other drugs including carbamazepine, valproate, and lamotrigine afterward came into being.

THEORY OF EPILEPSY

A neurological condition called epilepsy affects the brain and results in seizures or convulsions. A complex interaction of genetic, environmental, and neurological factors forms the basis of epilepsy.

The genesis of epilepsy is significantly influenced by genetic factors. Certain genes have been linked to a higher chance of getting epilepsy, according to studies. Seizures may result from anomalies in the brain's

physiology or structure caused by these genes.
Environmental factors can also contribute to the foundation of epilepsy. Prenatal factors, such as maternal infections or exposure to toxins, can increase the risk of epilepsy. Head injuries, infections, strokes, and brain tumors can also cause epilepsy.

The origins of epilepsy also include key neurological variables. Neurons in the brain exchange electrical signals with one another to communicate. These signals get messed up in epilepsy, which results in aberrant brain activity and seizures. Although the precise mechanisms causing these disturbances are not entirely known, they entail modifications to how neurons communicate with one another.

Overall, there are many different aspects to epilepsy, and there is a complicated interaction between hereditary, environmental, and neurological factors. For the development of successful treatments and strategies to manage epilepsy, it is essential to comprehend these aspects.

CHAPTER 2

Stories from patients with epilepsy who are living normally.

A neurological condition that affects the central nervous system is epilepsy. Mild to severe seizures are brought on by it. Every person may experience an unexplained seizure once in their lives. One might also develop as a result of a sickness or accident.

However, epilepsy is defined as experiencing two or more unprovoked seizures.

Treatment for epilepsy is available, and safety measures can minimize injury and seizure activity. In actuality, most epileptics lead full, regular lives, including these famous persons. See what these well-known epileptics have to say about their illness and see if you may find some motivation for yourself.

Theodore Roosevelt

While the 26th President of the United States was likely best known for his environmentalist efforts, Theodore Roosevelt also stayed active outdoors in the face of severe health issues. Among these were asthma, eye problems, and epileptic seizures. Roosevelt did not specifically address epilepsy because of stigmas and eugenic movements at the time he lived, but he did talk about overcoming obstacles. "Far better is it to dare mighty things, to win glorious triumphs, even though chequered by failure,… than to rank with those poor spirits who neither enjoy nor suffer much because they live in a grey twilight that knows not victory nor defeat." He also said, "Courage is not having the strength to go on; it is going on when you don't have the strength."

Indeed, anyone can be motivated by quotes like this. But they might be especially motivating for people who regularly struggle with particular problems, like epilepsy. Roosevelt had health issues, yet he was known for being active. All of his professional endeavors were ongoing throughout his lifetime.

Daniella's Epilepsy Journey

Daniella Brown has had both successes and setbacks in her life. She is a strong and driven person. She was raised in a little town, in a loving household, with ambitions and aspirations just like any other youngster. Daniella, however, was given an early diagnosis of epilepsy, a condition marked by recurring seizures.

Daniella fought through the difficulties of her health as a young kid with steadfast bravery. When she was just five years old, she had her first seizure, which caused her family to be concerned and unsure about her future. They sought the finest care and therapy for their daughter by consulting with medical professionals.

Daniella never let her epilepsy define her despite the hardships it brought. She approached each day with a contagious sense of excitement and an unbreakable spirit. She was encouraged by her family to pursue a proper education and never allowed her illness to impede her success. To give Daniella the safe and inclusive atmosphere she needed to succeed in school, her parents and teachers collaborated to do so.

Daniella struggled to control her epilepsy as a child. She religiously adhered to her treatment regimen, which included taking medication, going to the doctor regularly, and leading a healthy lifestyle. Daniella's seizures were unexpected, but she wasn't going to let that stop her. She learned how to see the warning signals and took preventative measures to guarantee her safety and those around her.

Despite her obstacles, Daniella achieved academic success and nurtured a love of reading and writing. She gave her all to her studies, frequently turning to the written word for comfort. Writing became her outlet, a way for her to communicate her ideas and feelings, as well as a way for her to get away from the occasional frustrations that epilepsy caused. As Daniella grew older, she started to promote education and awareness about epilepsy. She joined support groups and took an active part in activities and initiatives meant to lessen stigma and raise money for epilepsy research. To encourage other people who are experiencing the disease and to inform a larger audience about how epilepsy affects daily life, Daniella shared her personal story.

Through her advocacy activities, Daniella made friends with people from all walks of life and helped to create a close-knit group of people who were all affected by epilepsy. Her sense of purpose and belonging helped others embrace their journeys and face the difficulties epilepsy posed.

People in her immediate vicinity saw and admired Daniella's tenacity and tenacity. She served as an example to many people that having epilepsy did not preclude living a meaningful life.

She overcame her challenges and used them as stepping stones on the path to success thanks to her upbeat attitude and unyielding perseverance.

Although Daniella's experience with epilepsy had been difficult, she vowed not to let it define who she was. Instead, she accepted her illness and used it to spur individual and cultural transformation. Her experience serves as a reminder that anyone can overcome obstacles and have a successful life with willpower, encouragement, and an optimistic approach. Daniella Brown is a living example of the strength and potential of resiliency.

Danny Glover

Danny Glover has an impact on people when he talks about epilepsy, but he will always be remembered for his part in the well-known "Lethal Weapon" films. The Academy Award-winning actor experienced seizures and epilepsy as a young child. He outgrew his epilepsy, like many others who have the condition.

After experiencing his first seizure at the age of 15, Glover credits his ability to detect the symptoms of seizures with contributing to his success. He stated, "I could eventually see it happening...

Every time, I became a little stronger and the symptoms started to lessen until I was prepared to perform on stage. Today, Glover works to bring awareness to epilepsy by supporting the Epilepsy Foundation. He contributes to the organization's programs for children and volunteers his time speaking about epilepsy and bringing awareness to the issue.

Dai Greene

Dai Greene, a British track and field hurdler who competes in the Olympics, is a good example of how lifestyle choices can have a significant impact on your health. Greene suffers from epilepsy, but he hasn't had a seizure in years because he changed his lifestyle, cut out alcohol, and improved his diet.

Greene explained to The Guardian in 2011 how his family initially had doubts about the adjustments. But they were OK after I talked to my expert, who approved of my stopping my medicine because I'd drastically altered my lifestyle, he continued. Since I had stopped drinking, I was certain that I wouldn't place myself in a situation where I would experience another seizure. I now only occasionally consume alcohol. After the season, I've gone out drinking occasionally, but as long as I spend the day in bed, everything is good. Additionally, it helps that my girlfriend doesn't drink.

While Greene deserves praise for conquering these obstacles without the use of medicine, you shouldn't stop taking your prescriptions without first having a serious conversation with your doctor. Without first contacting a doctor, no one with a medical issue should rely solely on lifestyle modifications. But Dai's accomplishment demonstrates that leading a healthy lifestyle may be a fantastic addition to receiving expert medical care.

. Jason Snelling

Jason Snelling, a former running back for the Atlanta Falcons, is another significant ally of the Epilepsy Foundation. In college, he received an epilepsy diagnosis. With the help of therapy, he was able to play football once more and succeed as a professional athlete.

Snelling has been vocal about his illness, especially the stigmas and challenges associated with the diagnosis. He claimed in an interview that it took a while for the physicians to diagnose him since not all seizures are caused by epilepsy; they could instead be the result of another seizure illness. It did turn out to be epilepsy in my situation. He also offers guidance on stigma and fear: There is a great deal of anxiety associated with having seizures in public and maybe doing so in front of other people. And I frequently advise people not to stress out too much about that. You can continue doing whatever you want to do while managing your epilepsy. Epilepsy has strengthened my character because I was able to overcome a lot of obstacles and battle my worries.

Snelling now collaborates with the Epilepsy Foundation to raise awareness of the disease. By sharing his personal experiences, he reaches out to others. Additionally, he collaborates with the Foundation's Know the Difference program for African Americans. Snelling's outreach is assisting in raising money and awareness for this vital cause.

CHAPTER 3

UNVEILING THE ENIGMA

Bringing clarity to the mysterious world of epilepsy. Come along as we solve the puzzles and dispel the myths surrounding this complex neurological illness. Let's take this chance to educate ourselves on epilepsy and how to support individuals who are impacted by it. Together, we can make a difference!"

WHAT IS EPILEPSY

A neurological condition called epilepsy is characterized by frequent, unannounced seizures. Atypical electrical activity in the brain during seizures causes momentary disturbances in regular brain functions. All ages can be affected by epilepsy, which affects an estimated 50 million individuals globally.

Seizures can range in length, from brief attention lapses or twitches of the muscles to protracted convulsions and loss of consciousness. Depending on which area of the brain is being impacted by abnormal electrical activity, several symptoms might be felt during a seizure.

Based on elements including seizure type, age of start, and underlying etiology, epilepsy can be divided into several epileptic syndromes. There are numerous forms of seizures. Some epileptics may have a known underlying disease, such as a brain tumor, stroke, or genetic predispositions. The cause of epilepsy, however, is frequently unknown.

An extensive medical history, physical examination, and different tests, such as an electroencephalogram (EEG) to record the electrical activity of the brain, are typically required for the diagnosis of epilepsy. Antiepileptic drugs are frequently used as part of epilepsy treatment to prevent, control, or lessen the frequency of seizures. Surgery may be a possibility in some situations to remove the part of the brain causing seizures or to implant gadgets that help control brain activity.

People who have epilepsy may have difficulties since seizures can interfere with daily life and negatively affect the quality of life. However, many people with epilepsy may enjoy happy lives if they receive the right medical care and support. Working together with medical specialists to identify a suitable course of treatment and to create safety and seizure control plans is crucial for people with epilepsy.

HOW DOES EPILEPSY IMPACT LIFE

Recurrent seizures are a neurological disease known as epilepsy. These seizures, which can differ in kind, frequency, and strength, can significantly affect the lives of those who have epilepsy. The following are some effects that epilepsy can have on people's lives:

Effects on the body: Seizures can result in a variety of bodily symptoms, such as convulsions, unconsciousness, twitching muscles, and jerky movements.

These can cause accidents or falls that result in injuries, increasing the risk of fractures, head injuries, and other physical traumas.

Emotional and psychological impact: Epilepsy can take a toll on a person's emotional well-being. Individuals with epilepsy may experience fear, anxiety, depression, and low self-esteem due to the unpredictability of seizures and the potential social stigma associated with the condition. Coping with the emotional aspects of epilepsy can be challenging and may require support from healthcare professionals, family, and friends.

Lifestyle limitations: Epilepsy can impose limitations on a person's lifestyle. For example, driving restrictions may be imposed due to safety concerns. Certain activities, such as swimming alone, climbing heights, or operating heavy machinery, may also need to be avoided or done with caution. These limitations can impact independence, career choices, and overall quality of life.

Medication side effects: Anti-seizure medications are often prescribed to manage epilepsy. However, these medications can have side effects such as drowsiness, fatigue, dizziness, memory problems, and mood changes. Balancing the benefits of seizure control with the potential side effects of medications can be a delicate process, and adjustments to medication regimens may be necessary over time.

Social challenges: Epilepsy can present social challenges due to the misconceptions and stigmas associated with the condition. Some people may feel uncomfortable or fearful around individuals with epilepsy, leading to social isolation or exclusion. People with epilepsy may also face difficulties in education, employment, and relationships due to prejudices or misunderstandings about the condition.

Treatment management: Managing epilepsy requires ongoing medical care, including regular visits to neurologists and adherence to medication schedules. Additionally, individuals with epilepsy may need to track and report seizure activity, maintain a healthy lifestyle, and make accommodations to minimize seizure triggers. The demands of treatment management can be time-consuming and may require adjustments to daily routines and activities.

Despite the challenges, it is important to note that epilepsy can often be well managed with appropriate medical care and support. Many individuals with epilepsy lead fulfilling lives, pursue their goals, and find strategies to cope with the condition effectively. Support from healthcare professionals, support groups, and a strong network of family and friends can significantly contribute to managing the impact of epilepsy on daily life.

CHAPTER 4

Epilepsy and genetics

Genetics of epilepsy

Epilepsy is a neurological disorder characterized by recurrent seizures. Although the exact cause of epilepsy is not fully understood, there is evidence that genetic factors play a role in the development of epilepsy. Here is an overview of the genetic aspects of epilepsy:

Genetic predisposition:

In some cases, epilepsy can be caused by certain genetic mutations. These mutations can affect ion channels, receptors, or other proteins involved in neuronal function in the brain. Examples of genetic mutations associated with epilepsy include mutations in genes such as SCN1A, SCN2A, and DEPDC5.

Complex genetic interactions: Epilepsy is often considered a complex condition, meaning that multiple genes interact with environmental factors to contribute to its development. Several genetic variants such as single nucleotide polymorphisms

(SNPs) and copy number variations (CNVs) are associated with increased risk of epilepsy. However, the genetic makeup of epilepsy is highly heterogeneous, and different individuals or types of epilepsy may involve different genetic variants.

Genetic syndrome:
Some hereditary syndromes are strongly associated with epilepsy. In addition to seizures, these syndromes are often characterized by other physical and mental disorders. Examples include Dravet syndrome, Lennox-Gastaut syndrome, and tuberous sclerosis complex (TSC). In such cases, the presence of

specific genetic mutations or chromosomal abnormalities contributes to both epilepsy and its associated symptoms.

Genetic test:

Genetic testing can identify certain mutations or genetic variations associated with epilepsy. It helps diagnose epilepsy symptoms, identify underlying causes, predict prognosis, and determine treatment. Genetic counseling is often recommended for individuals and families considering genetic testing because it can provide information about inheritance patterns, risk of recurrence, and available treatment options.

Although genetic factors contribute to the development of epilepsy, it is important to note that they are not the sole determinants. Other factors, such as brain injuries, infections, tumors, and developmental disorders, may also cause seizures and contribute to the overall risk of epilepsy. Moreover, the interplay between genetics and environment is complex and not yet fully understood.

If you or someone you know has epilepsy, we encourage you to consult a medical professional, such as a neurologist or geneticist, who can provide customized information and guidance based on your specific situation.

Other causative factors of epilepsy

Although the exact cause of epilepsy is often unknown, several factors, in addition to genetic factors, may contribute to its development. These factors include:

Brain injury or trauma: Head injuries from accidents falls, and other traumatic events can cause epilepsy. The severity of the injury and the location of the affected brain can influence the risk of developing epilepsy. Brain tumors, stroke, and infections (such as meningitis and encephalitis) can also cause epilepsy.

Developmental disabilities: Some developmental disorders, such as neurofibromatosis, tuberculosis, and Down syndrome, increase the risk of epilepsy. These disorders are associated with abnormal brain development and can result in epilepsy as a symptom. Prenatal factors:

Epilepsy may be caused by factors that occur before birth. These include prenatal infections, maternal drug and alcohol abuse, and lack of oxygen during labor. These factors can affect fetal brain development and increase the risk of subsequent epilepsy.

Infection: Central nervous system infections such as meningitis, encephalitis, and brain abscess can cause epilepsy. These infections can cause inflammation and scarring in the brain and interfere with normal brain activity.

Stroke and Vascular Disease: A stroke is a disruption of the blood supply to the brain and can lead to epilepsy. Other vascular diseases, such as arteriovenous malformations (AVMs), which are abnormal tangles of blood vessels in the brain, can also cause epilepsy.

Metabolic Disorders:
Certain metabolic disorders, such as mitochondrial disorders and metabolic disorders, can lead to seizures and epilepsy. These disorders affect energy production and chemical balances in the brain, causing abnormal electrical activity.

It is important to note that in some cases epilepsy can develop without an obvious cause, and the specific cause may vary from person to person. Diagnosing the cause of epilepsy often requires a detailed medical history, physical examination, and sometimes brain imaging studies (MRI, CT) and EEG (electroencephalography) to assess brain activity. will require additional testing.

EPILEPSY SYNDROME

West Syndrome: This syndrome usually affects infants and is characterized by infantile spasms, short, symmetrical jerks of the body.

Dravet Syndrome:
This rare genetic disorder begins in infancy and includes several types of seizures, including prolonged seizures caused by fever (febrile seizures).

It is important to note that epilepsy manifests differently for each person, and some people experience a combination of different types of seizures. Proper diagnosis and classification of epilepsy types are important for determining appropriate treatment options. If you or someone you know is having a seizure, it's important to see a doctor for an accurate diagnosis and guidance on how to treat symptoms.

EPILEPSY SYMPTOMS

Epilepsy is a neurological disorder characterized by recurrent seizures. Seizures are the hallmark symptom of epilepsy and vary in appearance and severity. The specific symptoms experienced during a seizure depend on the area of the brain affected and the type of seizure. Common symptoms of epilepsy are:

Seizures:

Seizures can manifest in a variety of ways, including:

Generalized seizures:

They affect both sides of the brain and can cause loss of consciousness or convulsions (tonic-clonic seizures), dazed states (absence seizures), or short muscle spasms (myoclonic seizures).

Focal seizures:
These occur in specific areas of the brain and can lead to changes in behavior, emotion, sensory perception, or motor function. Simple partial seizures without loss of consciousness or complex partial seizures that can cause loss of consciousness.
AURA: Some people with epilepsy experience before a seizure

occurs. Auras are warning signs or sensations that precede a seizure and vary from person to person. Visual disturbances, auditory hallucinations, strange smells and tastes, dizziness, and other sensory changes may occur. **Unconscious:**Certain types of seizures can cause temporary loss of consciousness or fainting. **convulsions**: tonic-clonic seizure or grand mal seizure, is characterized by loss of consciousness and body rigidity (the tonic phase) followed by rhythmic jerky movements (the clonic phase). These attacks may be accompanied by drooling, tongue biting, and loss of bladder or bowel control.

Changes in consciousness or behavior: Some seizures can cause a change in consciousness, confusing, rigid seizures, unresponsiveness, or repetitive movements such as smacking lips or rubbing hands.

Sensory symptoms:A seizure may be accompanied by unusual sensations, such as B. Tingling or numbness in certain parts of the body, changes in vision, hearing unusual sounds, or experiencing unusual tastes or smells.

Emotional or psychological symptoms: Certain seizures can cause emotional or psychological symptoms such as severe anxiety or agitation, déjà vu, jambul (a feeling of being unfamiliar with a familiar environment), and hallucinations.

It is important to note that not all seizures are caused by epilepsy and may be caused by other factors such as high fever, head injury, or certain medical conditions. If you or someone you know is suspected of having epilepsy, it is important to see your doctor for proper evaluation, diagnosis, and treatment.

CHAPTER 5

seizure spotlight

Overview of Epileptic Seizures

What is an epileptic seizure?

An epileptic seizure is a sudden, temporary disturbance in the normal electrical activity of the brain. It is usually characterized by symptoms that range from mild sensations to loss of consciousness and seizures. Epileptic seizures are caused by abnormal electrical discharges in neurons in the brain.

What types of epileptic seizures are there?

There are many different types of epileptic seizures, which can be divided into two main categories: Focal (partial) and generalized seizures. Here's an overview of each type:

Focal (partial) seizures:

Focal seizures without loss of consciousness:

These seizures do not cause loss of consciousness. It can be further classified into two types:

Focal seizures with motor symptoms:
These seizures can cause involuntary movements such as B. Cramps and repetitive movements of the limbs.

Focal seizures with sensory symptoms:
These seizures are sensory experiences such as tingling, numbness, and hallucinations.

Focal seizures with impaired consciousness:
These seizures impair a person's consciousness and cognition. The person may appear dazed, confused, or absent-minded. They may also exhibit automatic

behaviors such as lip-smacking or repeating repetitive movements.

GENERALISED SEIZURE

Absence seizures:

These short seizures, also called petit mal seizures, occur mainly in children. It is accompanied by a sudden loss of consciousness, often accompanied by subtle body movements such as staring, winking, or lip-twitching.

Tonic seizures:

These seizures cause muscles to stiffen, causing the person to fall to the ground.

Clonic seizures:

Clonic seizures are characterized by rhythmic, repetitive jerky movements of the muscles.

Tonic-clonic seizures:
Formerly known as a grand mal seizure, this is the best-known seizure. These include a combination of muscle tension (tonic phase) and jerky movements (clonic phase). Loss of consciousness and confusion after a seizure are common.
Myoclonic seizures:
Myoclonic seizures are characterized by sudden, brief muscle spasms or spasms.
Cataplexy:

Cataplexy is a sudden loss of muscle tone that causes a person to fall or bow involuntarily.

It is important to note that everyone experiences seizures differently, and some people experience a combination of different types of seizures. Proper diagnosis and classification of seizures should be made by a doctor who specializes in neurology or epilepsy.

REFLEX SEIZURE

WHAT DOES REFLEX SEIZURE MEAN

Reflex seizures, also known as reflex epilepsy, are a type of seizure triggered by a specific sensory stimulus or activity. It is classified as a type of epilepsy because it involves recurrent seizures, episodes of abnormal electrical activity in the brain.

In reflex seizures, seizures are usually triggered by specific triggers or stimuli, such as B. Flashing lights, certain sounds, tactile stimuli, and even certain movements. These triggers vary from person to person, and what causes a reflex seizure in one person may not affect another. The exact mechanisms behind reflex seizures are not fully understood, but they are thought to involve the hyperexcitability of specific regions in the brain responsible for processing sensory information associated with stimuli. Seizures are thought to occur because susceptible people respond abnormally to these stimuli.

It is important to note that reflex seizures are relatively rare and account for only a small percentage of all epilepsy cases. Once diagnosed with reflex seizures, it is important to recognize and avoid certain triggers to minimize the risk of seizures. In addition, antiseizure drugs may be prescribed to manage and control seizures.

How are reflex seizures diagnosed?

Diagnosis of reflex seizures usually involves a combination of medical history, clinical judgment, and diagnostic tests. Here are the steps to diagnose reflex seizures:

Medical history:
Your doctor will take a detailed medical history to understand the pattern and characteristics of your seizures. They ask about specific triggers that keep triggering seizures, such as B. Flashing

lights, certain noises, reading, or certain movements.

Laboratory tests:

Your doctor will do a thorough physical and neurological examination to assess your general health and neurological function. This helps rule out other possible causes of seizures and detect additional neurological abnormalities.

Electroencephalogram (EEG):

Electroencephalography is an important diagnostic test for reflex seizures. In EEG, electrodes are placed on the scalp to record electrical activity in the brain. A person may be exposed to certain triggers (such as flashing lights) to induce seizures during an EEG. EEG helps identify abnormal patterns of brain activity, especially in response to stimuli.

Video EEG monitoring:
In some cases, advanced video EEG monitoring may be required. This is continuous EEG recording while the patient is video-monitored for an extended period, often in an epilepsy monitoring unit. This allows clinical signs and symptoms to be correlated with his EEG findings, thus helping to diagnose and classify seizures.

Additional tests:
Additional testing may be required in certain circumstances. These

include magnetic resonance imaging (MRI) and computed tomography (CT) to examine brain structures and rule out underlying structural abnormalities or lesions that may contribute to seizures. may include imaging studies.

Psychological evaluation:
In some cases, a psychological evaluation may be done to assess the person's cognitive and emotional functioning, especially if there is concern about the impact of the seizure on daily life.

Diagnosis of reflex seizures requires careful evaluation by an epilepsy specialist neurologist or epileptologist. Proper diagnosis is critical to determine the most appropriate therapeutic approach, including the use of seizure drugs, avoidance of triggers, and lifestyle changes to effectively manage symptoms.

Non-epileptic seizures

Seizures that are not considered epileptic seizures are called non-epileptic seizures or non-epileptic events. These phenomena, although superficially similar to epileptic seizures, are not caused by abnormal electrical activity in the brain. Instead, they are usually attributed to other underlying factors such as psychological or physiological conditions. Here are some examples:

Psychogenic non-epileptic seizures (PNES):
These seizures are often associated with psychological factors and may reflect psychological distress or trauma. Although PNES can resemble seizures, it is not caused by abnormal activity in the brain.
Focal neurogenic non-epileptic seizures (FND):
These phenomena resemble focal seizures but are not caused by epilepsy. These are thought to be due to functional or psychological factors rather than structural abnormalities in the brain.
syncope:

Fainting is a temporary loss of consciousness and muscle tension caused by a temporary reduction in blood flow to the brain. Although it is not an epileptic seizure, it may resemble an epileptic seizure. Fainting can have many causes, including heart problems and vasovagal reactions.

Sleep-related movement disorders:
These disorders are abnormal movements and behaviors during sleep, such as sleepwalking and sleep-related leg cramps. It may look like a seizure, but it has nothing to do with epilepsy.

Breath-holding spell:

Young children have seizures, often involuntarily holding their breath for a short time after bursting into tears. They are usually benign and are not considered epileptic seizures.

It is important to note that diagnosis of non-epileptic seizures requires a thorough medical evaluation by a physician. They consider several factors such as a person's medical history, symptoms, and diagnostic tests to distinguish between epileptic and non-epileptic events.

Seizure triggers:

Factors and controls

Factors that provoke epileptic seizures

It's important to note that epileptic seizures can be triggered by a variety of factors, and triggers can vary from person to person. Here are some common factors that may contribute to triggering epileptic seizures.

Lack of sleep:

Lack of sleep or poor sleep quality may increase the risk of seizures in some people. Adhering to a regular sleep schedule and getting enough rest is recommended.

Stress and Anxiety:

Mental stress, anxiety, and other strong emotions can trigger seizures. Relaxation techniques and stress management strategies can help minimize the effects of stress. Sensory stimulation:

Certain sensory stimuli such as flashing lights and patterns (photosensitivity), loud noises, and even certain visual patterns can trigger seizures in some people. This condition is called reflex epilepsy. Avoiding or minimizing exposure to these triggers may help.

Screen flickering and video games:

Rapidly changing visual stimuli, such as screen flickering or intense video games, can trigger seizures in people with photosensitivity. We recommend that you take regular breaks and use screens with adjustable refresh rates. Medication default or change:

Forgetting to take a drug, stopping it abruptly, or drastically changing the dose or type of drug without a doctor's supervision may increase the risk of seizures. It is important to follow the prescribed treatment plan and consult your doctor before making any changes.

Alcohol and drug use: Alcohol and certain recreational drugs can lower the seizure threshold and increase the chance of having a seizure. We encourage you to limit or avoid your intake of alcohol and illegal drugs.

Hormonal changes: Hormonal fluctuations, such as those that occur during a woman's menstrual cycle, may be associated with an increased risk of seizures. In some cases, hormone therapy may be recommended to treat this aspect of epilepsy.

Illness and Fever:

Certain illnesses, infections, and high fevers can cause attacks, especially in children. It is important to treat the underlying disease and promptly control fever with appropriate treatment.

If you miss a meal:

Low blood sugar due to skipping meals or irregular eating habits can increase the risk of attacks. A regular, balanced diet is essential.

Other factors:

In some cases, seizures can be triggered by certain environmental factors, allergies, heat, excessive exercise, or other personal factors. Tracking an individual's triggers by using a seizure diary or consulting with a medical professional can help identify and manage these factors.

People with epilepsy need to work closely with their healthcare team to identify specific triggers and develop strategies to minimize their effects. Because everyone experiences epilepsy differently, individualized care and treatment plans are essential for effective seizure control.

CHAPTER 6

epilepsy and related disorders

The relationship between epilepsy and anxiety
Although epilepsy and anxiety are two separate disorders, they often coexist and can affect each other. Here is some information about epilepsy and anxiety.

Epilepsy:
Epilepsy is a neurological disorder characterized by recurrent seizures. Seizures are caused by abnormal electrical activity in the brain and can cause a variety of symptoms depending on the area

of the brain affected. These symptoms may include loss of consciousness, seizures, muscle spasms, sensory changes, or temporary confusion.

ANXIETY

Anxiety refers to a mental health condition characterized by excessive worry, fear, and discomfort. People with anxiety may experience symptoms such as persistent tension, restlessness, irritability, difficulty concentrating, trouble sleeping, and physical symptoms such as a fast heart rate and sweating.

Coexistence:

Studies suggest that people with epilepsy are more likely to suffer from anxiety disorders than the general population. The relationship between epilepsy and anxiety is complex and varies from person to person. Possible reasons for comorbidity include the effects of chronic disease, uncertainty associated with seizures, side effects of antiseizure medications, or common underlying factors in the brain.

Effects on epilepsy:
Anxiety can affect epilepsy by increasing the frequency and severity of seizures. Stress and

emotional turmoil are known to trigger seizures in some people with epilepsy. Therefore, effective management of anxiety is important to minimize the risk of seizures.

Effects on anxiety:
Epilepsy can also contribute to anxiety symptoms. Fear of having a seizure in public or certain situations can lead to anticipation and specific phobias. In addition, side effects of antiseizure medications, such as mood swings and cognitive impairment, may contribute to anxiety symptoms. process:

Treatment of epilepsy and anxiety often requires a multidisciplinary approach. Antiseizure drugs are usually prescribed to treat epilepsy and may help relieve anxiety. However, in some cases, antiseizure drugs can make anxiety symptoms worse. It's important to work closely with your healthcare provider to find the right balance.

Psychological therapies such as cognitive-behavioral therapy (CBT) can help manage the anxiety associated with epilepsy. CBT helps individuals identify and challenge negative thought patterns, develop coping strategies, and gradually face fears and cues. Relaxation techniques, stress management, and lifestyle changes can also help.

If you or someone you know has epilepsy or anxiety, it's important to talk to your doctor for an accurate diagnosis and an appropriate treatment plan tailored to the person's specific needs.

The link between epilepsy and depression

Epilepsy and depression are two different ailments, but in some cases, they can coexist or even affect each other. Information about epilepsy and depression includes:

Epilepsy:

Epilepsy is a neurological disorder characterized by recurrent seizures. Seizures are caused by abnormal electrical activity in the brain. These attacks vary in intensity and appearance, affect different areas of the body, and cause different symptoms.

Epilepsy can have multiple causes, including genetic factors, brain injury, tumors, stroke, and infections.

 Depression: Depression, on the other hand, is a mood disorder that affects a person's emotional health, thoughts, and behavior. It is characterized by persistent sadness, hopelessness, and lack of interest or pleasure in activities. People with depression experience changes in their appetite, sleep patterns, energy levels, and concentration, and may think about hurting or killing themselves.

Epilepsy and Depression:

There is a complex relationship between epilepsy and depression. Studies show that people with epilepsy may be at a higher risk of developing depression than the general population. The reason for this association is not fully understood, but several factors may contribute.

Biological factors:
Epilepsy and depression may share biological mechanisms in the brain. Chemical imbalances, such as abnormalities in neurotransmitters such as serotonin, can contribute to both diseases.

Psychological factors:
Living with epilepsy can be difficult and stressful. The unpredictability of seizures, social stigma, and limitations in daily life can cause emotional distress and increase the risk of depression.

medicine:
Some anti-seizure drugs used to treat seizures can have side effects that affect mood and increase the risk of depression.
Social isolation:
People with epilepsy can face social isolation due to misunderstandings and discrimination about their

condition. Lack of social support and loneliness can lead to depression.

It is important to note that not everyone with epilepsy develops depression, and not everyone with depression develops epilepsy. However, if you or someone you know is experiencing any of the symptoms, it's important to seek professional help. A neurologist, psychiatrist, or mental health professional can provide the appropriate diagnosis, treatment, and support for your individual needs. Treatment options may include medications, psychotherapy, lifestyle changes, and support groups.

Epilepsy and cerebral palsy

Epilepsy and cerebral palsy are two different neurological disorders that can occur together or independently. Here's an overview of each condition:

Epilepsy:
Epilepsy is a neurological disorder characterized by recurrent seizures without a cause. Seizures are caused by abnormal electrical activity in the brain, causing temporary changes in behavior, sensation, and consciousness. Epilepsy can occur at any age and can have many causes, including brain

injury, genetic factors, infections, and structural abnormalities in the brain. It can also be a sequela associated with other neurological disorders such as cerebral palsy.

Cerebral Palsy:

A cerebral palsy is a group of permanent movement disorders caused by damage to the developing brain, usually before or during birth. It affects muscle tone, posture, and movement control, leading to difficulties with coordination, balance, and motor skills. The severity of cerebral palsy varies from person to person and ranges from mild to severe disability. The disease may be accompanied by other comorbidities such as epilepsy, mental retardation, speech, and hearing impairments.

The relationship between epilepsy and cerebral palsy is complex. Some people with cerebral palsy have epilepsy, some do not. People with cerebral palsy are at a higher risk of developing epilepsy than the general population. The presence of both conditions may further complicate management and treatment approaches, as the symptoms and treatment goals of each condition may interact or overlap.

Getting proper medical care and treatment is very important for people with either or both symptoms. Addressing the unique needs of people with epilepsy and cerebral palsy often requires a multidisciplinary approach involving neurologists, pediatricians, physical and occupational therapists, and other professionals. Treatment options may include medication, physical therapy, assistive devices, and other supportive measures tailored to each individual's unique circumstances.

CHAPTER 7

Research progress

About three-quarters of people diagnosed with epilepsy can control their seizures with medication or surgery. However, even with the best treatment, about 25 to 30 percent continue to have attacks. Doctors call this treatment-resistant epilepsy. In some cases, a type of seizure called status epilepticus occurs. A seizure lasting more than 5 minutes or recurring without regaining consciousness. Prolonged status epilepticus can damage the brain and be life-threatening. The U.S. federal government supports research to better understand epilepsy and reduce the burden of epilepsy through improved treatment and prevention. Much of this research support is provided by the National Institutes of Health (NIH). The National Institute of Neurological Disorders and Stroke (NINDS) is the NIH's lead laboratory for epilepsy research. Several other NIH laboratories also fund epilepsy-related research. Representatives of the NIH laboratories, the Centers for Disease Control and Prevention (CDC), the Department of

Defense, the Department of Veterans Affairs, and the U.S. Food and Drug Administration (FDA) provide communication and coordination between agencies and agencies that fund epilepsy-related research. We are collaborating through the Interagency Alliance for Epilepsy Research (ICARE), which was established to promote capacity. In 2000, NINDS and epilepsy research and advocacy organizations co-sponsored a White House-initiated conference, "Curing Epilepsy: Focus on the Future." The conference has been viewed as a turning point for research on epilepsy by shifting the focus from treating seizures to identifying cures, defined as "no seizures, no side effects, and the prevention of epilepsy in those at risk." The first Epilepsy Research Benchmarks grew out of the momentum created by this conference, as a way to communicate and address important research priorities and as a framework for periodically "benchmarking" progress. A second conference in 2007, "Curing Epilepsy: Translating Discoveries into Therapies," reassessed the state of research on epilepsies and revised the Epilepsy Research Benchmarks, adding emphasis to the conditions that co-occur with epilepsies and sudden unexpected death in epilepsy (SUDEP). A third conference in 2013, "Curing the Epilepsies: Pathways Forward" provided an update on the state of research and will result in another revision of the Benchmarks.

Today, more than a decade since they were first developed, the Benchmarks are increasingly embraced by the entire epilepsy community, including NIH, researchers, and professional and advocacy organizations. While the ultimate goal of curing epilepsy has not yet been achieved, researchers have made substantial progress. Epilepsy research has led to exciting advances in all areas of benchmarking.

Develop new therapeutic strategies and optimize existing treatments

Several important advances in diagnostics, therapeutics, and technology are approved or in varying stages of approval in the US and Europe. New chemicals are being developed for treatment-resistant epilepsy. For example, Ezogabine (also known as Retigabine) was approved by the US Food and Drug

Administration (FDA) in 2011 for the prevention of partial-onset seizures through a novel mechanism of action. Several other potential drugs and compounds (brivaracetam, perampanel, YKP3089, VX-765) are in development, also aiming to prevent seizures by novel mechanisms. In addition, some active substances are approved for specific seizure types or syndromes.

Rufinamide (Lennox-Gastaut syndrome), stiripentol (Dravet syndrome), adrenocorticotropic hormone, also known as ACTH (infantile convulsions), and vigabatrin (infantile convulsions).

mTOR inhibitors (such as everolimus) are being tested for the treatment of tuberculosis complex (TSC) attacks and other conditions. The drug Everolimus is approved by the FDA to prevent tumor growth in TSC patients. Determining the best monotherapy for childhood absence epilepsy (CAE), the most common childhood epilepsy syndrome is evolving, occurring in 10-17 percent of all children with epilepsy. CAE patients tend to have multiple seizures each day. To find medications that limit exposure to drug-related side effects, researchers compared ethosuximide, lamotrigine, and valproic acid for treating CAE. Ethosuximide proved to be the best monotherapy due to the optimal balance between efficacy and relatively few side effects.

NINDS-funded researchers have made great strides in improving treatment for people with status epilepticus. Treatment of such long-lasting attacks can be particularly difficult because it is difficult to establish an intravenous (IV) line when an attack occurs. Results from a randomized controlled trial known as the Pre Arrival Rapid Anticonvulsant Administration Trial (RAMPART) showed that seizures were significantly more frequent in people given midazolam by autoinjector than in those given intravenous lorazepam. to indicate that it stopped early. The auto-injector is similar to the EpiPen drug delivery system used to treat serious drug reactions. Fewer hospitalizations due to faster recovery from attacks.

Ongoing basic research efforts continue to identify targets for therapeutic development. For example, research has focused on the role of gamma-aminobutyric acid (GABA), a key neurotransmitter that inhibits central nervous system activity.

Other studies have explored ways to block the activity of the excitatory neurotransmitter glutamate.

Epilepsy has so many different underlying mechanisms that it is unlikely that a single treatment will be developed. Instead, management approaches should be tailored to specific syndromes.

Sidebar:
Anticonvulsant Screening Program
In 1975, NINDS established the Anticonvulsant Screening Program (ASP) to facilitate the development and evaluation of

new antiepileptic drugs. At that time, the pharmaceutical industry had little incentive to support epilepsy research in the development of therapeutic agents. Since its inception, ASP has helped bring new antiepileptic drugs to market by providing researchers with a common platform for standardized testing of potential therapeutics in animal models. The resources available to researchers through ASP can save years of development time.

ASP priorities are aimed at preventing the onset of epilepsy, altering the course of the disease, finding treatments for cases unresponsive to currently available therapies, and identifying epilepsy subtypes and their unmet needs. have evolved to focus on developing therapeutics that ASP maintains a database of over 30,000 submitted compounds, and plans are underway to improve the usability of the data for researchers tracking new compounds. NINDS continues to look for new ways to improve ASP. New tests and procedures are being developed and implemented to significantly expand the sensitivity of conventional screening approaches to identify new pharmacotherapies targeting the most unmet medical needs in epilepsy.

surgery

Surgery remains an effective option for patients with treatment-resistant epilepsy. The most common surgery is to remove the seizure focus, the small area of the brain where seizures occur. In very serious cases, surgeons perform an operation called "multiple subpial transections". This includes incisions designed to prevent the spread of seizures to other parts of the brain while preserving the person's normal abilities. Doctors may also perform a surgical procedure called a corpus callosotomy (cutting the nerve fibers that connect the two hemispheres of the brain) or a hemispherectomy (removing one half of the brain). Researchers continue to refine surgical techniques to make them less invasive and prevent cognitive and other neurological deficits that can result from surgery. New imaging techniques are important advances in identifying the effects of surgery and minimizing adverse events. Many epilepsy centers have begun using functional magnetic resonance imaging (fMRI) to "map" language and memory zones before surgery.

NIH-funded researchers hope to validate that fMRI improves surgical outcomes and standardizes best practices for its use.

Researchers are also investigating how to combine imaging modalities to more accurately map language zones. For example, one study used diffusion tensor imaging (DTI) together with fMRI and magnetoencephalography (MEG), another magnetic-field-based brain-mapping technique, to assess preoperative language processing and to assess temporal lobe epilepsy. Preserving major language zones during surgery. There is evidence that high-frequency oscillations (HFOs) measured in the neocortex and temporal lobe can be biomarkers of epileptic networks and thus may be useful in surgical mapping and predicting outcomes after epileptic surgery. Retrospective studies have shown that the removal of HFO-producing zones is associated with improved outcomes after surgery. His minimally invasive MRI-guided laser surgery is being investigated for the treatment of epilepsy associated with tumors such as hypothalamic hamartoma and tuberculosis complex. In this technique, a very small hole is made in the skull through which a thermal laser is inserted to remove epileptogenic areas under MRI guidance.

New imaging techniques are important advances in identifying the effects of surgery and minimizing adverse events. Many epilepsy centers have started using functional magnetic resonance imaging to "map" language and memory zones before surgery.

Brain Stimulation

Electrical stimulation of the brain remains an interesting therapeutic strategy. Types of stimuli include:

Deep brain, intracranial cortex, peripheral nerves, vagus nerve, and trigeminal nerve. To date, deep brain stimulation has involved either the thalamus or the hippocampus, and one large clinical study tested only thalamic stimulation.

A clinical study of deep brain stimulation in the anterior thalamic nucleus showed a significant reduction in seizures over time, with the majority of participants experiencing benefits. Thalamic stimulation is approved for use in Europe but not in the United States.

Trigeminal nerve stimulation reported efficacy rates similar to vagus nerve stimulation, with about half responding (responders defined as a 50 percent or greater reduction in seizure frequency). Although seizure freedom has been reported with both methods, it remains rare.

NINDS-supported researchers are developing methods to predict seizures by analyzing patterns of brain activity before seizures begin. One promising application of this research is the development of implantable devices that can detect impending seizures. When an implanted device is detected, it will perform interventions such as electrical stimulation or fast-acting drugs to prevent seizures from occurring. First-generation seizure control devices in clinical trials use such seizure prediction technology. The NeuroPace RNS system is one of a group of devices called responsive stimulation or closed-loop devices.

Optogenetics is a new experimental technique that may lead to future generations of closed-loop devices. This involves the genetic delivery of light-sensitive proteins to specific populations of brain cells.

Photosensitive proteins are inhibited or stimulated by exposure to fiber optic light. Although optogenetic methods are not currently used in humans, such an approach may enable targeted modulation of network excitability, providing a means of intervening at or before the onset of seizures. there is a possibility.

Diet: The high-fat, very low-carbohydrate ketogenic diet is a long-standing treatment for drug-resistant epilepsy, but in recent years there has been renewed interest in how it works. This diet is effective in reducing seizures in some people, especially children with certain types of epilepsy. Studies show that more than 50 percent of people who try a ketogenic diet experience 50 percent or more improvement in seizure control, and 10 percent experience seizure freedom. However, some people find it difficult to continue with the prescription.

Researchers are trying to figure out exactly how the ketogenic diet prevents seizures. They hope to find a way to mimic the anti-seizure effects without dieting. The research has increased our understanding of the link between energy metabolism and neuronal excitability and may contribute to a better understanding of how a ketogenic diet promotes seizure control.

Additionally, researchers are working on improved versions and alternatives to the ketogenic diet. For example, studies show promising results for the modified Atkins diet and the low glycemic index diet, both of which are less restrictive and easier to follow than the ketogenic diet. However, well-controlled randomized controlled trials have not yet evaluated this approach, and many questions remain about the optimal circumstances for its use.

Researchers are trying to figure out exactly how the ketogenic diet prevents seizures. They hope to find a way to mimic the anti-seizure effects without dieting. Research is advancing our understanding of the relationship between energy metabolism and neuronal excitability.

Gene therapy and cell therapy
The discovery of genetic mutations associated with certain epilepsy syndromes has raised the possibility that gene-directed therapy can be used to counteract the effects of these mutations. Gene therapy continues to be the

subject of numerous studies in animal models of epilepsy, and the number of possible approaches continues to grow. A common approach in gene therapy research, called transfection, uses modified parts of viruses to introduce new genes into brain cells, which act as "factories" for the production of potentially therapeutic proteins. Works.

Several proteins were selected for transfection. Animal studies have shown that it is possible to introduce new proteins into cells and in some cases associated reductions in seizure frequency, duration, and severity. Cell therapy differs from gene therapy in that rather than introducing genetic material, whole cells are transplanted into the brain. For example, in animal studies, NINDS-funded researchers controlled seizures in mice by transplanting a special type of neuron that produces the inhibitory neurotransmitter GABA into the hippocampus of the mouse brain. succeeded in

Gene and cell therapy remain attractive and promising strategies for treating and potentially curing some types of epilepsy. However, their progress as viable therapeutic options in humans requires new techniques and methods that can target specific neurons in the brain. Such an approach should be able to bring about more sustainable change. The virus is introduced into brain cells, which act as "factories" that produce potentially therapeutic proteins.

Prevent epilepsy from developing
Until recently, the development of treatments for epilepsy has focused primarily on treating seizures in people who already have epilepsy. In addition to efforts to develop new and improved anti-seizure treatments, researchers are now also working to prevent epilepsy in at-risk populations.

Measures that reduce the risk of head injuries and trauma - such as B. Improving vehicle safety and the use of seat belts and bicycle helmets - can prevent epilepsy associated with traumatic brain injury. Good prenatal care, such as treating high blood pressure and infections during pregnancy, can prevent brain damage in the developing baby, which can lead to epilepsy and other neurological problems later in life. Treating cardiovascular disease, high blood pressure, infections, and other disorders that affect the brain in adulthood and old age can also prevent some types of epilepsy. Although such measures can prevent brain injury from occurring, there are currently no known interventions that specifically reduce the risk of seizures after brain injury. None of the available antiepileptic drugs have been shown to affect the development of epilepsy in humans. Researchers are working to change that.

Recent animal studies have helped elucidate the mechanisms of seizures associated with hypoxic-ischemic encephalopathy (HIE) (caused by a lack of oxygen in the brain) and potential therapeutic strategies in neonatal clinical trials. starting to evaluate. This includes single medications, combinations of medications, or combined medications with cooling strategies targeted at her infant with HIE for epilepsy prevention. Adenosine is an inhibitory neuromodulator thought to promote sleep and suppress wakefulness. Studies in animal models have shown that increased levels of adenosine in the brain suppress the development of spontaneous recurrent seizures after the initial injury.

Epilepsy monitor:
Wearable and implantable devices are being developed to monitor brain activity and detect seizures and the onset of red flags. The purpose of these devices is to enable timely intervention and improve the quality of life for people with epilepsy.

CHAPTER 8

living with epilepsy

Strategies for Coping with Epilepsy

Here are some coping strategies that can help people with epilepsy:

Take your medicine as directed. Consistent use of prescribed anti-seizure medications can prevent seizures and minimize the severity of seizures.

Stress management:

Stress can trigger seizures in some people with epilepsy, so it's important to find healthy ways to manage stress. Techniques such as meditation, deep breathing, and regular exercise may help.

Get enough sleep:
Lack of sleep can trigger seizures. Establishing a regular sleep schedule and getting enough rest is important. Avoid triggers:
Some people with epilepsy have specific triggers that can trigger seizures, such as flashing lights or certain noises. Avoiding these triggers can help reduce the risk of seizures.

Keep a seizure diary:

Keeping track of when seizures occur and what triggers can trigger them can help identify patterns and make epilepsy easier to manage.

Wear a medical alert bracelet. Wearing a medical alert bracelet helps emergency responders understand a patient's condition and provide appropriate treatment if needed.

Find support:

Living with epilepsy can be difficult and having a support system in place is important. Joining a support group or seeking professional advice can provide emotional support and help you manage your stress.

It is important to note that coping strategies may vary from person to person, depending on the severity of epilepsy and individual needs. Individual consultation with a doctor is recommended.

Safety Precautions in Epilepsy

People with epilepsy need to take certain safety measures to reduce the risk of seizures and minimize potential harm. Here are some general safety precautions to consider.

Medication Compliance:

Make sure the patient is taking the prescribed antiepileptic drugs as directed by the doctor. Consistent use of drugs is essential to treat epilepsy and reduce the frequency of seizures.

Periodic medical examination: Schedule regular appointments with the patient's neurologist or epilepsy specialist to monitor the patient's condition, adjust medications as needed, and address concerns.

Lifestyle changes: Encourage patients to adopt a healthy lifestyle, including regular sleep patterns, a balanced diet, stress management strategies, and avoidance of triggers such as alcohol, drugs, and excess caffeine.

Home security:
A. Prevents tipping over. Eliminate tripping hazards, use non-slip mats on floors, and install handrails on stairs.
 B. Bathroom safety: Install handrails in bathrooms and non-slip mats in showers and bathtubs.
C. Kitchen Security: Use safety locks on ovens and stoves to prevent accidental burns and fires.
D. Electrical security:

Make sure power cords and appliances are in good condition and do not overload outlets.

Seizure precautions:

A. Clear the area.
Remove any sharp or hard objects that may pose a hazard during a seizure.

B. Soften the area:
Use padded furniture or place cushions on the floor to reduce the chance of tipping.

C. Stay close to you:
Don't hug people during a seizure, stay close to them to provide support and prevent injury.

D. Pad Head:
Place a soft pillow or rolled towel under your head to protect

yourself from impact with hard surfaces.

e. Seizure time:
Note the duration of the seizure and call emergency services if the seizure lasts longer than usual or if this is your first seizure.

 Public safety:
A. Please let others know:
Inform family, friends, colleagues, and teachers of the patient's condition and what to do during an attack.

B. Medical ID:
Encourage patients to wear a medical alert bracelet or necklace detailing their epilepsy diagnosis and emergency contact information.

C. Driving restrictions:
Follow local laws regarding driving prohibitions for people with epilepsy.

It is important to consult a doctor, preferably a neurologist or epileptologist, for individualized advice and guidance on how to treat epilepsy and how to implement appropriate safety precautions.

Legal Rights in Epilepsy

Epilepsy is a neurological disorder characterized by recurrent seizures. People with epilepsy have legal rights to protection from discrimination and equal opportunities in many areas of life. While details of legal rights may vary by jurisdiction, we can provide some general information about legal rights commonly associated with epilepsy. For accurate and up-to-date information, we always recommend that you consult an attorney or advocacy group familiar with the laws of your particular jurisdiction. Here are some important legal rights that relate generally to epilepsy:

Protection against discrimination:

People with epilepsy are protected from discrimination in many areas such as employment, education, housing, and public services. Employers, educational institutions, and landlords generally have to make reasonable accommodations for the full participation of people with epilepsy.

Employment rights:
People with epilepsy are usually protected from discrimination in the workplace. Employers are generally prohibited from making employment decisions based solely on a person's epilepsy, so long as the person can perform

essential functions of the job with or without reasonable accommodation. Reasonable accommodation may include flexible working hours, changes in work assignments, or provision of necessary medical equipment.

Right to education:
Students with epilepsy are entitled to adequate housing and support at their educational institution. This may include changes in classroom settings, additional testing time, access to medications, and having staff trained to respond to seizures.

Driving Permit:

Licensing laws for people with epilepsy vary by jurisdiction. Depending on the location, people with epilepsy may be required to meet certain criteria, such as B. Being seizure-free for a while before you can get or renew your driver's license. It is important to familiarise yourself with the specific laws and regulations in your jurisdiction.

Health insurance coverage: In many countries, health insurance companies are prohibited from denying coverage or charging higher premiums just because you have epilepsy. It is important to read the terms of your health insurance to understand what coverage is available for epilepsy-related treatments and medications.

Data protection and confidentiality: Medical information, including epilepsy diagnosis and treatment, is subject to privacy. Healthcare providers must maintain the confidentiality of patient information and must not disclose information without the patient's consent except in certain cases permitted by law.

Please note that legal rights and protections may vary by jurisdiction. It is advisable to consult with legal professionals or advocacy organizations specializing in disability rights or epilepsy-related issues to get accurate and up-to-date information specific to your situation.

Epilepsy Support Group

Advocacy and support groups play a crucial role in raising awareness, providing information, and offering support to individuals and families affected by epilepsy. If you're interested in starting or joining an advocacy and support group focused on epilepsy, here are some steps you can take:

Research existing groups: Start by researching if there are any epilepsy advocacy and support groups already established in your area. Look for local and national organizations that work towards epilepsy awareness, education, and support.

Connect with established organizations:

Reach out to existing epilepsy organizations to inquire about their work and see if there are opportunities to collaborate or volunteer. They may have resources, materials, or events you can participate in to raise awareness and offer support. Create a group.

If you can't find an existing group in your area or would like to start a new one, consider starting your own advocacy and support group.

Start by finding interested people who share your passion for epilepsy education and support. Connect with people through local hospitals, clinics, support groups, online forums, and social media platforms.

Define goals and objectives. Determine the purpose and goals of your advocacy and support groups. Are you primarily focused on raising awareness, providing emotional support, organizing events, or advocating for policy change? A clearly defined goal helps guide the group's activities.

Set up recurring meetings.

Groups can meet regularly to discuss plans, share information, and support each other. These meetings can be face-to-face or virtual, depending on group member preferences and availability.

PR & EDUCATION:
Organise events, workshops, and seminars in your community to raise awareness of epilepsy. These efforts will help educate the public about epilepsy, reduce stigma, and provide resources for those affected. Consider working with medical professionals, local schools, and community centers to reach a wider audience.

Online Presence:

Create an online presence for interest groups and support groups. Websites and social media pages serve as platforms for sharing information, resources, personal stories, and upcoming events. It can also provide an opportunity for people to connect with your group and seek support.

Support services:

We provide a variety of support services for people with epilepsy and their families. This may include providing helplines and support hotlines, arranging support group meetings, and connecting individuals to resources such as educational materials, medical providers, and legal advice.

Work with your health care professional:
Build partnerships with medical professionals who specialize in epilepsy. Working with neurologists, epileptologists and other medical professionals provides the group with valuable insight, support, and guidance.

Advocacy efforts:
Consider participating in advocacy to promote policies that support people living with epilepsy. This may include working with

policymakers, participating in legislative activities, and raising awareness of issues affecting the epilepsy community.

Remember, it takes time and effort to build and maintain interest and support groups. By building strong networks, nurturing professional relationships, and consistently working toward goals, groups can make a positive impact on the lives of people suffering from epilepsy

THE IMPORTANCE OF PROPER DIAGNOSING AND TREATMENT

Diagnose & Treat Epilepsy!

Hello, defenders of health and recovery! Let's take a moment to highlight a crucial issue that demands all of our focus: the astounding significance of correctly identifying and treating epilepsy.

Understanding the complexity of epilepsy rises tall as a beacon of hope in a world where information empowers us. Millions of people struggle with epilepsy, which can cause unpredictable seizures at any time. But worry not, for as medicine advances, diagnosis turns into our strong sword and treatment into our impregnable shield.

Imagine a situation where each person with epilepsy gets a prompt and accurate diagnosis, enabling them to make informed decisions. Imagine a world where personalized treatment programs enlighten patients' paths and open up new avenues for opportunity. That's the kind of world we want to build.

The right diagnosis is the first step on the path to success. Medical specialists solve the complex mystery of epilepsy using cutting-edge technologies and their extensive knowledge, much like accomplished detectives. They carefully and compassionately examine each person's particular neurological patterns, searching every avenue for solutions.

Why is accurate diagnosis important? because it lights the home fire. It prepares the ground for specialized therapies that let patients take back control of their life and achieve new heights. The options range widely from anti-seizure drugs and lifestyle changes to cutting-edge therapy. We create a canvas of resiliency, boldness, and revived dreams with each well-constructed strategy.

However, this battle calls for far more than just the expertise of medical wonders. It needs a village, a unified front of assistance and comprehension. Together, we can vanquish the stigma that surrounds epilepsy and replace it with empathy, acceptance, and knowledge. Let's advocate for the cause by spreading knowledge and creating a network of kindness that will show the way to a better future.

Let's move forward together, determined to give epilepsy sufferers more control. Let's honor the unsung heroes—the doctors, nurses, and patients who fight this illness with unrelenting courage. To unlock the potential for many lives to blossom, let us never waver in our dedication to accurate diagnosis and treatment.

Always keep in mind that epilepsy will submit to us when we stand together. We will overcome the difficulties it brings with precise diagnosis and treatment and bring out a world abounding with hope, resiliency, and unflinching drive.

Let's all work together to bring about change and illuminate the way to a better future!

CHAPTER 9

EMBRACING THE LIGHT

A message to those who suffer from epilepsy

Brighten up your journey:
Bright Hope for Epilepsy Warriors!
Amazing souls in the epilepsy
community.
We want you to know that you are
absolute superheroes who face
each day with unwavering
strength and resilience. Living with
epilepsy can be uniquely
challenging, but your spirit shines

like a lighthouse and inspires us all.

In the unpredictable ups and downs of life, I want you to remember that you are never alone on this journey. Together, we'll wrap you in warm embraces and build a support network that will empower you to overcome hardships.

Remember that epilepsy is only part of your story, not the whole story. Your true character transcends any diagnosis and radiates courage, determination, and an indomitable joie de vivre.

You have strong resilience that has the power to illuminate even the darkest moments. Embrace that unique radiance within you. Because that light has the potential to brighten the lives of those around you. Her journey is a testament to human fortitude and the triumph of hope over adversity.

Never forget the strength within you as you overcome winding roads. Celebrate victories big and small by tapping into your inner warrior and being kind to yourself. Reach out to the epilepsy community and share your experience, knowing that your voice has immense power and that understanding and compassion fosters.

Together, we strive for a future where epilepsy no longer overshadows life, where stigma disappears, and where hope reigns. Until then, remember that your light is precious and can create ripples of change in the world.

So epileptic warriors, keep smiling! We will stand by you and cheer you every step of the way. you are never alone. Because we are a united force united in compassion and solidarity.

A Message to Families of Epilepsy Patients

a dear loving family,

You are a beacon of strength and resilience in a world where the complexities of epilepsy are often difficult to comprehend. Your unwavering love and support for your loved ones battling this disease is simply amazing. Today, I want to honor your extraordinary journey and remind you of the incredible impact you have made on the lives of people living with epilepsy.

You have created a haven of understanding, empathy, and compassion within your family. The courage they show as they navigate the untrodden seas of epilepsy is truly inspiring. Despite all the ups and downs, you remain resolute, reaching out for help or giving a comforting hug when needed.

Due to its unpredictable nature, epilepsy is often overshadowed by anxiety and fear. But it is only in your loving embrace that those shadows disappear and are replaced by a ray of hope and unrelenting optimism. They are the foundation upon which hope is built, reminding loved ones that they are never alone in their struggle.

Before you, laughter triumphs over tears, resilience triumphs over adversity, and solidarity overcomes all the challenges epilepsy brings. The family becomes a sanctuary where everyone feels valued, supported, and encouraged to pursue their dreams and aspirations, even in the face of obstacles.

Through unwavering love, you teach the world the true meaning of acceptance and understanding. You break down prejudices and misconceptions and pave the way for a more inclusive and caring society. Your actions have an impact far beyond your own home, inspiring others to embrace differences and offer support to those in need.

On this journey, it's important to remember the importance of self-care, both for people living with epilepsy and for the whole family. You are a warrior, and warriors take time to regain their strength. Find comfort in each other's presence, share the burden when it gets heavy, and seek solace in the simple pleasures life has to offer.

Know that your love and support can make a huge difference in the life of your loved one with epilepsy. The resilience, compassion, and unwavering spirit you demonstrate every day are the true embodiment of a great family. Your unwavering commitment inspires us all to stand by your side and promote a world where epilepsy is understood, accepted, and overcome with grace. May your family continue to shine brightly, radiating love and hope to all who face similar challenges. Your story is a tale of strength, unity, and undying love that touches us all deeply.

SUMMARY

In summary, this book takes us into the complex and fascinating world of epilepsy. From our historical understanding of the disease to current state-of-the-art treatments, we have examined the many challenges facing people living with epilepsy.

We have seen how epilepsy can affect people of all ages and backgrounds and the impact it has on their lives. We learned about different types of seizures and the importance of proper diagnosis and treatment.

Most importantly, it has increased my understanding and compassion for people with epilepsy. We have learned to appreciate their courage and resilience and accompany them in their fight against this disease.

We must continue to raise awareness for people with epilepsy and advocate for better research and treatment options. We must strive to build a world in which everyone can live a full and meaningful life, regardless of their condition.

This book is a journey of discovery, but it is also a call to action. Support and empower people with epilepsy and work together to build a better and more inclusive future for all.

thank you

ACKNOWLEDGEMENT

Writing a book on epilepsy has been an incredibly enlightening and fulfilling journey, and I am deeply grateful to everyone who helped and contributed to the making of this book. With our heartfelt gratitude, we salute the individuals and organizations that have made this effort possible.

First of all, I would like to express my sincere gratitude to all people living with epilepsy and their families who have shared their stories, experiences, and insights with me. Your courage, resilience, and determination have always served as a source of inspiration and it is your strength that motivates me to continue working towards a better understanding of epilepsy. I extend my deepest gratitude to the medical professionals and researchers who have dedicated their lives to the study and treatment of epilepsy. Her tireless efforts to advance scientific knowledge and improve the lives of people suffering from epilepsy are admirable. We appreciate your willingness to share your expertise and provide valuable guidance throughout the writing process of this book.

We would like to thank the epilepsy organizations, support groups, and foundations that work tirelessly to raise awareness, provide resources and bring a sense of community to individuals and families affected by epilepsy. Your dedication to making a difference is truly remarkable and it has been an honor to work with so many of you. I am grateful to my friends and family for their unwavering support and encouragement. Your trust in me and my work is invaluable, and I appreciate your patience, understanding, and love throughout this writing process.

I would like to thank the publishing team who believed in the importance of spreading knowledge about epilepsy and worked diligently to bring this book to the world. Your professionalism, expertise, and dedication helped shape the final product.

Finally, I would like to thank all the readers of this book. It is my sincere hope that the information contained in these pages will increase our understanding of epilepsy, defuse misconceptions, and promote a more inclusive and supportive society for people living with epilepsy.

We would like to express our sincere gratitude to all of the above, and to all of you who have contributed in some way, big or small. Your support, guidance, and encouragement have greatly contributed to the creation of this book, and I am most grateful for your presence in my life.

With deep gratitude.

www.ingramcontent.com/pod-product-compliance
Lightning Source LLC
Chambersburg PA
CBHW061633250726
48659CB00004B/1190